HERBS AND DRUGS INTERACTION

WHY YOUR MEDICATION IS NOT EFFECTIVE

BY ESTHER ADEBAYO

TABLE OF CONTENTS

Introduction
Chapter 1 - REASONS PEOPLE TURN TO HERBAL DRUGS.
Chapter 2 - RISKS & DANGERS INVOLVED IN THE USE OF HERBAL DRUGS.
Chapter 3 - Kava
Chapter 4 - Sage
Chapter 5 - Flaxseed
Chapter 6 - Hawthorn
Chapter 7 - Licorice
Chapter 8 - Milk thistle
Chapter 9 - Curcumin
Chapter 10 - Danshen
Chapter 11 - Cranberry
Chapter 12 - Goji berry
Chapter 13 - Evening primrose oil
Chapter 14 - Echinacea
Conclusion

Introduction

Traditional medicine has evolved to become Herbal medicine, the uses and study of plants as medicine. You have probably heard of herbal medicines – or even used them in one form or other, at least once. Tea, leaf, herbs, shrubs, and spices are examples of forms of plant-based herbal remedies. You may even have used a herbal product such as a nutritional supplement.

There is a steady growth in the acceptance of herbal medicines, but the two words - Herbal and Medicine" used together are enough to make many doctors react with a certain level of skepticism. Yet it is impossible to deny the increase in the use of herbal drugs worldwide in the past thirty years or so. In some countries, herbal drug usage has outweighed the use of prescription drugs. Later on in this book, we shall discuss in detail the causes of the rise in the use of herbal drugs, these reasons range from affordability, culture and beliefs, intense marketing by sellers, nature lovers, healthy lifestyle, and the desire to avoid the harsh side effects of some clinical drugs.

The main area of focus is the complications that may arise when herbal drugs are taken without caution or consideration of pre-existing conditions, dosage, allergies, contraindications, and compatibility or interaction with other prescription medications.

There is a reason many regulatory bodies have cautioned against uninformed use of herbal medicines without prior consultation of medical professionals. Most people who use herbal drugs do not seek a doctor's advice and examination to assess any pre-existing conditions that may lead to further complications. Yet another danger zone is the use of herbal drugs while taking a different prescribed medication. A physician unaware that a patient has been taking an herbal remedy to treat a particular sickness may prescribe medication that will react negatively with the herbal drug, resulting in complications and - in worst-case scenarios - death.

Later on, we will discuss twelve popular herbal drugs you should never mix with certain prescription drugs. The benefits, side effects, interaction, and reaction with specific medications. We will also discuss the popular use of herbal drugs to mitigate the withdrawal symptoms of addictive medical drugs and why that could also be a major risk.

There has been growing acceptance of the use of herbal drugs as alternative medicine in many developed countries, including the US, the UK, and Australia. While some countries, such as the UK, have accepted herbal medicine as an alternative for decades, others have taken decades to do so. The growing use of herbal medicine has brought about a more positive attitude by the medical profession towards the acceptance of herbal drugs, and the growing knowledge on the nature-based benefits of many of the drugs. For instance, in 2011 the European Union made it easier for European herbal drug sellers to import, manufacture and sell the drugs as long as there was a public information system that helped users make more informed decisions. However, not much emphasis has been put on the side effects and matters relating to the interaction between herbal drugs and other drugs.

The fact that there are no controls in place in many countries poses a risk factor. There is no standardization of use or prescriptions, no measurable units, nor generally accepted dosage, action, and side effects. Another reason is that herbal drugs are considered as a "home remedy" and therefore many users do not find it necessary to consult with their doctors on any herbal drugs they are taking. After all, they believe, herbal drugs are natural and natural means harmless. As we shall find out, herbal drugs used wrongly or alongside other medication can lead to serious health complications and even death.

If you have been a user of herbal drugs or are likely to do so, this may be one of the most important books you ever read on the good and the bad of herbal drugs and how you can avoid the bad so you can get the best out of them. Chapter 3 to 14 covers 12 popular herbs, easily available, common, and used by millions of people worldwide either as tea, spices, herbs, nutritional supplements, or food. The herbs covered in this book include kava, sage, flaxseed, hawthorn, licorice, milk thistle, curcumin, Danshen, cranberry, goji berry, evening primrose oil, and echinacea

Chapter 1 - REASONS PEOPLE TURN TO HERBAL DRUGS.

For centuries, herbal medicines have provided the remedy for many illnesses. However, with the emergence of tougher diseases and breakthroughs in the medical field and research, people have been introduced to prescription drugs, most of which, though slow in development and effectiveness have proven to work in the long run. In recent times, however, people seem to be reverting to herbal remedies. Let's take a look at some of the reasons for this sudden resurgence in the use of herbal drugs.

Financial reasons

Compared to conventional medicine, herbal medicine has proven to be cheaper in terms of its cost, thus making it more available to people who require the medication. It has gain traction in the treatment of terminally ill patients. The cost of treatment for terminal illnesses is quite high when using the hospital or conventional means.

While it is true that prescription drugs are expensive, it is also true that every human being has a right to proper healthcare regardless of their financial status, thus the option for seeking herbal treatment options.

Cultural and Beliefs

Herbal drugs are viewed as more compatible with people's beliefs worldviews or ideologies in many parts of the world

Herbal drugs have for centuries been used to cure diseases. They are part and parcel of many cultures, like in Asia and Africa. This makes them the priority for many cultures as people have interacted with them for a long time – especially in developing countries. There are "known and trusted" remedies for some of the ailments for illnesses long before the introduction of conventional medicine. This makes herbal medicines more trusted. For example, herbs such as ginger root, turmeric, lemon, and garlic have long been known as remedies for flu long before the introduction of prescription medicines such as cetirizine and Piriton (Chlorphenamine maleate) among others.

Herbal medications give users more control over such things as dosage and offer more autonomy and control over healthcare decisions. Some people find the prolonged usage of prescribed drugs to be tedious, while they accept flexibility with herbal drugs.

Unlike prescription drugs, many herbal drugs have additional health benefits that consumers find very attractive. For example, some herbs are also spices that can be used in preparing delicious meals or easily incorporated into daily activities like having an herbal tea in the evening.

The good thing about herbal drugs is that most of them are naturally grown. Some herbal drugs have brought with them attractive benefits, especially in cosmetology. Acne, among other skin-related conditions, has troubled many people. The non-herbal options in cosmetics carry adverse effects with them: involuntary skin lightening, wearing out the melanin level, and exposure to skin conditions like skin dryness and harmful sunburns when the skin layer is weakened. Herbal medicine/drugs provide better solutions, including skin rejuvenation and nutrition-based skin treatments.

Aloe Vera for example has been long known as a wonder plant. It has been used to traditionally treat conditions such as flu, stomach-related issues among others. When it comes to beauty therapy, the wonders of Aloe Vera are well witnessed in skin rejuvenation, softening, hair treatments among other benefits. These benefits are evident to the users and transcend beyond the brand name.

Goji berries are known to promote healthy skin among other benefits as they contain beta-carotene, a widely used ingredient in skin care creams.

Aggressive marketing, incentives, and word-of-mouth selling by herbal drug marketers and users.

People tend to believe in word-of-mouth more than the promised benefits of any product. The herbal drug users give firsthand evidence concerning the usage of certain drugs. According to the evidence given, the benefits are well visible, making them attractive for any prospective buyer.

Kava, for instance, is a popular herbal drug used to relieve pain and as a muscle relaxant.

Sage is believed to lower blood sugar levels, full of antioxidants, and lowers bad cholesterol levels. We shall discuss these among others – why people opt for these herbal drugs and why caution should be taken depending on underlying circumstances and interactions with prescribed drugs.

For respiratory illnesses such as pneumonia, for example, people will tend to listen to the effective medicines used by others. The locally assembled herbal medicines such as eucalyptus, fenugreek tea among others are well shared. The recipes for other herbs such as ginger root, turmeric, garlic, lemon, and honey are widely shared. Those herbal products produced by herbal companies are aggressively marketed and sell in droves. A prospective buyer will opt for the drug that s/he has seen someone close use and gets better. Royal jelly, cordyceps among other herbs are recommended for respiratory conditions such as bronchitis. The herbal companies market these herbal drugs with such amazing benefits and offer that any buyer cannot resist.

Take other examples such as memory loss and night blindness. Herbal drugs that are marketed are lecithin and calcium.

These herbal drugs are marketed as food supplements which prove very effective in the containment of these diseases.

Fear of side effects brought about by prescription drugs.

Have you listened to a medication advertisement on TV or radio recently? The list of possible side effects is such a long list, it outweighs the positive action of the drug. Anything can go wrong! Most prescription drugs, though effective, carry several side effects. Antibiotics, for example, leave most users feeling nauseous. Other prescription drugs if taken regularly can lead to addiction and body resistance. This means that one's body can reject them. For gynecological problems, most prescription drugs carry a ton of effects - such as hormonal imbalance, exposure to cervical cancer, irregular cycles, and even infertility or early menopause to some extent. These effects are unknown or reduced drastically by the use of herbal drugs. Herbal remedies ' side effects aren't adverse plus they provide better solutions to these health issues and more; better immunity. Yet mixing these herbal drugs with the drugs prescribed by the doctor can lead to more harm than good.

Many users believe that Dong Quai is good for the irregular menstrual cycle as well as premature menopause, and yet if used with other drugs that could be the beginning of a new problem. Other herbs such as papaya, hibiscus tea also help with fertility issues.

Ease of accessibility.

Unlike many conventional medications, herbal medicine is readily accessible. One can find herbs on the farm or even in the grocery store. It is also easier to buy a herbal drug online than a prescribed drug. The accessibility of herbs has been made easier by the fact that most of the best herbs are used for culinary purposes. Better still, these herbs are effective when ingested both raw and when cooked.
Trees such as eucalyptus and plantain leaves provide a good remedy for pneumonia yet they are in almost every home.

Some have proven to be more effective.
Compared to conventional medicine, some herbal drugs have proven more effective regarding the healing process. Studies have shown the therapeutic effect of milk thistle in the management of type 2 diabetes.
According to the studies, Milk thistle contains antioxidants which is why it acts on diabetes. Milk thistle also improves insulin resistance in Type 2 diabetes patients. This has proven more effective compared to prescription drugs for handling such illnesses.
Researchers have discovered that licorice root also contains substances with an anti-diabetic effect. These Amorfrutins are potent antidiabetic compounds that exist in natural products like licorice. Licorice not only reduces blood sugar, but they are also anti-inflammatory and are very well tolerated.
Cranberry is a herb that is widely used in the management of UTIs, slowing cancer progression, enhancing oral health among others.
More of these herbs and their effectiveness later in the book.
This is good proof of the effectiveness of herbal medicines.

The belief that herbal drugs are harmless
Many people believe that herbal drugs since they are made from plants or plant products are harmless. As discussed below, there are several risks connected to the use of herbal drugs. This is one of the main reasons users tend to use herbal drugs without giving much consideration to dosage or any reactions with other (clinical) drugs. One of the main reasons regulatory bodies have cautioned people on the uninformed use of herbal medicine based on heresy is that people tend to assume that no harm can come out of the use of these drugs. As a result, most people throw caution to the winds and are always chasing after the next herbal drug. Many of these drugs have never been tested and the only thing to hold on to is the seller's claim.

Dissatisfaction with conventional treatment

Some people give up on prescription drugs and opt for herbal drugs, especially if they do not see immediate or encouraging results. In some cases, they opt for herbal drugs to escape the long-lasting side effects of drugs like antibiotics. When one's body rejects one type of antibiotic, the patient is often introduced to a different, stronger antibiotic. If that doesn't work, another even stronger antibiotic is used. Antibiotics kill bacteria without sparing the normal floral that exist in the gut, leading to more complications and accumulation of medicine residue in the body which eventually results in body resistance- a very bad side effect.

Whereas for herbal medicine, results are visible in a matter of a few hours or days, it shows why herbal drugs are considered a better option by many compared to herbal drugs

Mistrust of practitioners and prescriptions

Some people have a problem trusting doctors and prescriptions and feel safer with herbal drugs. Sometimes this is caused by a bad experience with prescribed or over-the-counter drugs or a past misdiagnosis. Patients with allergic reactions to some prescribed drugs may also opt for herbal drugs.

Growing credibility

It has been a long journey, but herbal drugs have been gaining credibility and worldwide acceptance. This has encouraged people who would not have attempted this option ten or twenty years ago to feel comfortable using herbal drugs.

Chapter 2 - RISKS & DANGERS INVOLVED IN THE USE OF HERBAL DRUGS.

Herbal medicine, though effective, can be risky at times. It has to be considered that even if a drug is effective, it may have side effects. Therefore, herbal medicines as drugs either have side effects or are ineffective.

Here are some of the risks involved in the use of herbal drugs.

Lack of a precise recommended dosage.

Most herbal drugs are taken without the direction of the herbalist and have vague instructions, unlike prescribed medicine. Thus, it's very easy for them to be taken in an overdose. This might cause harm to the patient.

An example is Licorice: when taken in a small dosage it may not be harmful. However, if you are over forty and have a history of high blood pressure or heart disease, more than two ounces of licorice a day for two weeks can lead to the worsening of your condition.
If taken without proper research, herbs may cause harm to the fetus in case one is pregnant. Hibiscus tea, rosemary tea, dong Quai among other herbs can even serve as abortifacients if used without proper guidance from a specialist.
For proper effectiveness of herbal drugs as well as avoidance of adverse side effects, proper prescription by a qualified herbalist or herbal specialist is highly recommended.
Some herbal drugs react with prescription drugs especially when taken together.
Herbal medications and supplements may interact in harmful ways with the over-the-counter or prescription medicines you are taking. Taking herbal supplements may decrease the effectiveness of other drugs you are taking or may increase the negative side effects. It may also increase the activity of the prescribed drug, giving an overdose effect.
For example, people who use the blood-thinning drug warfarin (Coumadin) are cautioned against sudden increments in the intake of cranberries.
Digoxin (Lanoxin) helps the heart beat more strongly. Danshen also seems to affect the heart. Taking Danshen along with Digoxin can increase the effects of Digoxin and increase the risk of side effects. Do not take Danshen if you are taking digoxin (Lanoxin) without talking to your healthcare professional. (More on Danshen in following chapters).
One should talk to their medical practitioner before using herbal drugs with over-the-counter medicine as well as prescription medicine. This helps reduce the risks associated with mixing herbal medicine and prescription drugs. Many patients shy away from giving details of all over-the-counter remedies they are taking, to be documented as a reference, and considered by the doctor and pharmacy before prescribing and releasing prescribed medication.

Some herbs have been found to have toxins that can cause allergies and other health issues.
Herbal medicines may produce negative effects such as allergic reactions, rashes, asthma, headaches, nausea, vomiting, and diarrhea that can range from mild to severe. Like other prescription medications, herbal medicine should always be prescribed by a qualified and registered practitioner.

Some are counterfeit

Some herbal suppliers are just after making a profit. People should therefore purchase herbal drugs from reputable suppliers to avoid introducing more harmful components such as mercury into one's body.

Some herbs may contain toxic ingredients that may cause harm to one's body.

Plants have toxins in their chemical compositions that may cause harm to consumers. This is why specific parts of a plant are used. Although medicinal plants are widely used and assumed to be safe, they can potentially be toxic, especially during pregnancy. Where poisoning from medicinal plants has been reported, it has, in many cases, been due to misidentification of the plants in the form in which they are sold, or incorrect preparation and administration by inadequately trained personnel. Therefore, herbal drugs should preferably be administered by trained personnel.

Risk of drug contamination.

Hygiene is key in the handling of any product. Once hygiene is not considered during the preparation, storage, and supply of herbal drugs, contamination is an inevitable risk. Contamination may range from chemicals or microbiological contamination. Once these enter into any patient's system, they may cause adverse effects. There should be strict instructions on every prescription box about the storage of medicine for consumption – which is not always the case. Some herbal drugs have very little information on the packaging, and some herbal drug sellers (especially those who sell through third parties) do not take care to ensure proper storage is adhered to until the drugs reach the consumer. Once these conditions aren't met, the medicine can be easily contaminated. This could cause bodily harm to any patient under this prescription.

Untested herbs.

Evening primrose oil has been said to care for several health conditions. One of the outstanding benefits is the fact that it can be used in a situation of prolonged labor. This, however, hasn't been medically proven. The research done so far hasn't proven the safety during pregnancy or breastfeeding, thus it cannot be recommended. The bottom line is that more research needs to be done on many herbal drugs to back up the word of mouth and sellers' claims with approved laboratory testing methods and a wide scope of case studies.

Some pre-existing conditions react with herbal drugs.

We shall discuss this at length in the following chapters. Sage, for example, when taken in excessive dosage may trigger a potentially severe drop in blood sugar, leading to hypoglycemia. People with impaired kidney function are also cautioned about the consumption of sage.

Kava root herb is not recommended if one has liver disease, is pregnant or breastfeeding, or has depression or bipolar disorder. More of this will be discussed in-depth later in the book.

In a nutshell, herbal drugs, though mainly considered safe, should be taken with caution and proper guidance from a herbal specialist. Again emphasis must be put on this: If you are on other prescribed medicine you should alert your doctor on any alternative drugs you are taking, and that is mainly herbal medicine.

Herbal medicines are slowly but surely taking over prescription medicines. More people are starting to see the value of herbal medicines and are turning to them. A lot of prescription drugs have many severe side effects, chemicals, and addictive properties. That is why more people are turning to natural supplements to alleviate some of their ailments. Here is a breakdown of some of these herbal medicines, their usage, side effects, and drug interactions.

Chapter 3 - Kava

If stress or insomnia is taking a toll on you and you have trouble sleeping, Kava herbal medicine is a great remedy. Kava is an extract of the Piper methysticum plant. The medicine is considered an anxiolytic due to its calming and euphoric effect. Traditionally, Kava was used during certain religious and cultural ceremonies to hypnotize celebrants. The main medicinal properties of Kava are;

It helps to reduce anxiety and stress. It has been proven effective through a study conducted in 2013. The medicine has a relaxing quality that helps calm the nerves and anxiety level of anyone who takes it.

It helps to induce sleep for people suffering from sleeping disorders. It is difficult to sleep with your mind in turmoil. Kava has a relaxing effect that can help one sleep. However, there is no proven evidence to show that it can treat sleep disorders entirely.

It also helps to improve brain function. A clinical trial proved that taking a dose of the Kava extract can help to improve the performance, accuracy, and memory retention of the brain.

People who suffer from drug addiction can use Kava to reduce their cravings and urges to use drugs. One pilot study claims kava releases dopamine to the brain, which has an anti-craving effect. This finding, however, is based on one study. More research is needed.
Research also shows that daily usage of Kava helps to alleviate postmenopausal symptoms such as hot flashes and depression.

Despite its benefits, Kava is not entirely safe. There are a couple of research findings that show that the use of kava can have several side effects. As it is, Kava is illegal in some countries like Switzerland, Canada, France, and United Kingdom. It is still legal in the United States, however, people are still advised to use it with caution. are

The cons to taking kava;
Research has shown that Kava can lead to the damage of liver cells. It has hepatotoxic qualities that can cause abnormal enlargement of the liver. The symptoms are exhibited by fatigue, fever, abnormality in enzyme levels, and jaundice.
Prolonged usage can also lead to heart defects, eye problems, yellowing of the skin, and a dry itchy scalp.
Side effects
Most adults can use Kava drugs, however, some are at more risk of experiencing the side effects than others. Those at more risk are;
Pregnant women and nursing mothers. They are especially advised to stay away from the medicine as it is believed it can be passed to the child.
People with Parkinson's disease. It is also believed to worsen the symptoms of Parkinson's disease.
Since it also creates a state of altered consciousness, people who operate heavy machinery are advised not to use it or those who plan to drive.
The neurological effects of Kava are yet to be determined so people with mental disorders are cautioned against using the medicine.
People who suffer from any liver problems are also cautioned against using Kava. Kava can further damage the liver worsening the condition.
People who are scheduled to undergo a surgical procedure should also not take kava. Kava increases the effectiveness of anesthesia hence one can stay under for far too long.

Interaction and reaction

Kava interacts with many prescription medicines. It either reduces or increases the effectiveness of these drugs. Some of the drugs it interacts with are;
Alprazolam – Same as Xanax, this drug causes drowsiness in people who take it which is the same effect Kava has, when taken together, it becomes too much.
Sedatives – Sedatives are meant to help a person relax and they also cause sleepiness, but when taken with Kava, they may cause someone to oversleep and be constantly drowsy.
Levodopa – Levodopa increases dopamine in the brain while kava decreases dopamine in the brain. Taking Kava alongside levodopa decreases its effectiveness.
Liver medications – Kava slows down the speed at which the liver breaks some medications, which may reduce the effectiveness of these drugs. Kava might also increase the manifestation of side effects from these medicines. Liver medications include; imipramine, mexiletine, tacrine, and fluvoxamine.

Chapter 4 - Sage

If you know about herbal drugs, you may have heard about the healing effects of sage. The sage leaf has largely been turned into medicine to help treat the symptoms of diabetes, high cholesterol, Alzheimer's, and even menopause. Here is an in-depth analysis of its benefits;

Benefits

In people suffering from mild Alzheimer's, the properties of two sage species (Spanish sage and common sage) are mixed to help improve memory retention, learning capabilities, and the brain capacity to process information.
It helps to lower blood sugar levels in people suffering from diabetes.
Taking sage for some time also helps to reduce the symptoms of menopause such as hot flashes and sweating at night.
If you have high cholesterol levels, taking sage for 3 months greatly helps to lower low-density lipoprotein and triglycerides.
It also helps to protect the skin from skin redness after exposure to ultraviolet rays. Apply an ointment containing sage and it will alleviate the symptoms.

However, when taken in high doses by mouth for a long time it becomes unsafe. It is best to mix it with foods or take it in medicinal amounts. Common sage also contains the chemical Thujone which is poisonous and can cause damage to the nervous system and the liver. Additionally, it can lead to seizures.

Side effects

Sage is not a safe option for everyone. Certain individuals below are highly cautioned against taking it;

Pregnant women are highly advised not to use sage because the chemical properties present in it could lead to a miscarriage. Thujone induces menstrual flow which can lead to a miscarriage.

Nursing mothers are also advised against using it because it lowers the milk supply.

Women who have hormone-related conditions are also advised not to use sage and it worsens the condition. Sage increases the female hormone estrogen hence can worsen hormone-sensitive conditions. Such conditions include ovarian cancer, breast cancer, endometriosis, uterine cancer, and fibroids.

Thujone chemical present in sage also triggers seizures hence anyone with a seizure disorder is advised against using it.

Individuals with blood pressure problems are also advised against using sage. Different types of sage species can either increase blood pressure or decrease it. Spanish sage increases blood pressure while common sage lowers blood pressure.

If you are scheduled for surgery, you are also advised to stop using sage at least two weeks before your surgery date.

Interaction and reaction

Sage medicine interacts with some pharmacy medicines.

Antidiabetics - Sage reduces blood sugar levels so do antidiabetic drugs; taking them together can cause the sugar level to go too low. Examples of antidiabetics are glyburide, chlorpropamide, glimepiride, and insulin among others.

Anticonvulsants - Sage also reduces the strength of such drugs as phenobarbital, valproic acid, phenytoin among others. These are drugs used to prevent seizures, sage reduces their effectiveness hence one may experience more seizures.

Sedatives - Additionally, it interacts with sedatives and depressants such as zolpidem, clonazepam, lorazepam among others. Sage itself causes drowsiness, so taking it with sedatives may cause one to oversleep. It is important to let your doctor know if you are planning on taking Sage with other medications so they can advise you accordingly.

Chapter 5 - Flaxseed

Have you ever tried flaxseed in your food? Flaxseed comes from the crop flax and is currently available as seeds, powder, tablets, and even capsules. It contains some nutrients, hence it is used as a dietary supplement. It helps manage cholesterol levels, prevent diabetes, constipation, heart disease, and most importantly, cancer. So how does it work to benefit the body?

Benefits

Flaxseed contains antioxidants that help to prevent many diseases. The antioxidants slow the growth of tumors. Tumors grow by forming new blood vessels; taking flax seeds prevents this from happening. Omega 3 acid contains alpha-linolenic acid (ALA) which reduces any inflammation of arteries and hence reducing tumor growth.

Flaxseed contains Omega-3 fatty acids that inhibit cancer growth, as well as lignan that has estrogenic and antioxidant properties that lower the risk of contracting certain types of cancer.

Omega-3 also plays a big part in keeping the heart healthy; the nutrient lignan present in flax seeds helps to prevent cardiovascular diseases. Studies have proven that more people who take ALA present in flaxseeds have reduced chances of heart problems.

It also helps to manage cholesterol levels by preventing the intestines from absorbing cholesterol. Additionally, it prevents cholesterol from being deposited in the heart's blood vessels.

For those suffering from any kind of arthritis, or lupus, it helps to ease joint pain and stiffness. Flaxseed also contains an insoluble fiber content that helps to manage blood sugar levels in people with diabetes. For people with lupus, it helps to prevent inflammation of the kidneys when taken whole.

Studies have shown that flaxseed has the potential to prevent hot flashes for women going through menopause.

They also contain a good amount of fiber that when digested helps to alleviate constipation. However, it should still be taken with plenty of water otherwise it may only worsen constipation.

It is also a very good source of vitamins and minerals hence a good healthy diet. The body does not produce ALA, which is a good source of fatty acids. For people who do not eat fish or vegetarians, it is good to use flaxseeds to get omega -3 fats. Flaxseeds are also a good source of protein.
It can also be used to aid weight control for people who find themselves constantly hungry. Adding flax seeds to your beverage helps to reduce hunger pangs which in turn can help one control one weight.
Flaxseed can be used to manage blood pressure. For people who have high blood pressure, taking flaxseed daily can help to reduce blood pressure levels.

Side effects
Flaxseeds also have their downsides. Here are some of the disadvantages of taking flaxseeds.
When eaten raw or unripe, they can poison someone as they contain toxic compounds.
Flax seeds can block the intestines as it contains laxative effects, hence there is a need for them to be taken alongside plenty of water. When not taken with enough water they can also intensify constipation.
It can lead to gastrointestinal side effects such as diarrhea, pain in the abdomen, bloated stomachs, gas, stomach ache, and nausea.
So who should stay away from flaxseeds?
Pregnant mothers and nursing mothers are highly advised not to use flax seeds. Some reports show that flaxseed might harm the baby but there is not enough clinical evidence to prove this.
Women who have hormone-sensitive breasts or suffer from uterine cancer are also advised against using flax seeds.
People with bleeding disorders are cautioned against using flaxseeds as it slows down blood clotting which increases the risk of bleeding.
People who suffer from gastrointestinal obstruction should stay away from flax seeds as it can only make their symptoms worse due to their high fiber content.
Flaxseed also increases triglyceride levels hence people whose triglycerides levels are already high should stay away from flaxseeds

Drug interactions

Anticoagulants – these are medications that reduce blood clotting. When taken with flaxseeds it increases the risk of bleeding or bruising. For example, naproxen, aspirin, diclofenac, dalteparin, heparin among others.
Antidiabetes – for those taking antidiabetes medications to lower blood sugar levels, when taken alongside flaxseed it might extremely lower the blood sugar levels which is bad for the body. Examples are glimepiride, tolbutamide, glipizide, insulin among others.
It also interacts with any drugs that fall under the nonsteroidal anti-inflammatory drugs (NSAIDS). This is because the flaxseed itself also contains anti-inflammatory properties.
It also interacts with cholesterol-lowering drugs as it is also used to manage cholesterol levels.
Speak to your doctor first if you fall under these conditions or are on these types of drugs before using flax seeds. Add your grounded flax seeds to smoothies, stew and soup, salads, breakfast cereals, and yogurt. Start by adding small amounts before adding with time.

Chapter 6 - Hawthorn

The leaves, flowers, and leaves of the hawthorn plant are used as medicine. The hawthorn plant is used to treat various heart diseases – including congestive heart failure and irregular heartbeat. It can also be used to treat chest pains, atherosclerosis, manage high and low blood pressure, and also reduce high cholesterol levels. Below is a list of its benefits to the body;
Benefits
It widens the blood vessels, thus making it easier for the heart to pump blood out when it contracts. It also relaxes the blood vessels through the component proanthocyanidin which helps to alleviate the symptoms of blood pressure.
Hawthorn fruit also helps to manage cholesterol levels by preventing the liver from accumulating fats, excreting bile, and also activating the low-density lipoprotein receptors. It increases the formation of bile which in turn reduces the formation of cholesterol.
Additionally, the hawthorn plant is used to treat certain digestive issues such as stomach pain, diarrhea, and indigestion which can cause heartburn. For women suffering from menstrual complications, it can be used to ease such symptoms.

Hawthorn can be used as a sedative to allay anxiety in people who suffer from it. Furthermore, it helps to treat intestinal infections and tapeworms.

Research has shown that some products of the hawthorn plant seem to improve the symptoms of heart failure.

Lastly, it helps to soothe itching, frostbite, sores, boils, and ulcers when applied to the skin.

Side effects

Hawthorn has several side effects when taken. Different people experience different symptoms after taking Hawthorn. Some of the side effects include;

nose bleeding

lack of sleep

fatigue

migraines

lightheadedness

nausea

agitation

Who should not take hawthorn?

The effects of hawthorn on pregnant women and nursing mothers are yet to be determined hence they are advised not to take hawthorn. It is better to be safe than sorry.

Children are also not advised to take the medicine and adults are cautioned against taking it for a long period.

For those who plan on going into surgery, it is best to stop taking hawthorn two weeks before surgery. This is because it slows the clotting of blood putting someone at the risk of excessive bleeding during the process of surgery.

Drug interactions

Digoxin - Hawthorn interacts with digoxin which is a drug that is used to increase the strength of the heartbeat. Hawthorn also affects the heartbeat and this can cause certain side effects.

Nitrates - Since Hawthorn increases the flow of blood to the heart; taking it with nitrates which also increases blood flow can result in lightheadedness. Some of the nitrates include nitro-bid, nitro-stat, and nitroglycerin.

Blood pressure medications - It also interacts with medications for blood pressure such as nifedipine, isradipine, diltiazem, and verapamil. These medications lower the blood pressure while hawthorn does the same and this can incredibly put someone at risk.

Medications for sexual dysfunction - It should also not be taken alongside Viagra pills. This is because certain medications for sexual dysfunction decrease blood pressure while hawthorn does the same. This can make blood pressure levels fall too low.

Chapter 7 - Licorice

The licorice herb is native to Asia and Europe. The root of the plant is what is used as medicine. Licorice has been known to treat hepatitis, eczema, sores in the mouth amongst other ailments. Here is how it works;

Benefits

It contains chemicals that secrete a thin mucus, decrease the symptoms of a cough and help to hear the body of ulcers. Some licorice products contain antacids which when taken for about 4-16 weeks helps to heal stomach ulcers.

For those with canker sores in the mouth, gurgling water that contains licorice helps to alleviate the pain and reduce the size of the canker sores. One should gurgle a solution containing licorice to help with the sores.

Licorice gel can also be used to treat symptoms of eczema which is characterized by inflammation of the skin, redness, and itching. When the gel is applied to the affected area three times daily for at least two weeks, it helps to soothe these symptoms.

When one starts experiencing symptoms such as heartburn and acid reflux, taking an extract from the root of the licorice plant helps to relieve these symptoms.

It helps to treat the after-effects of using a breathing tube. Patients who have to use a breathing tube should take licorice lozenges or gurgle solutions with licorice to prevent soreness of the throat and coughing after tube removal.

Studies also show that the root properties can be used to treat respiratory conditions such as asthma.

Another research shows that certain licorice components can be used to treat hepatitis when taken intravenously.

Licorice also helps to reduce high potassium levels in people who have diabetes and kidney diseases.

Licorice can be used to reduce certain post-menopausal symptoms such as hot flashes.

Early research done on the benefits of licorice showed that it can help reduce tremors in people who suffer from Parkinson's disease, however, more research needs to be done to prove this.

Side effects

As is many other herbal medicines, licorice root has its side effects. Licorice root contains glycyrrhizin. A concentrated amount of glycyrrhizin causes fluid imbalances and increases electrolyte levels. Other effects of accumulated glycyrrhizin are; paralysis, heart attack, irregular heartbeat, low potassium levels, and increased blood pressure.

Additionally, it can lead to kidney failure

It can also cause erectile dysfunction in men by lowering the levels of testosterone.

Here's who should stay away from licorice root;

Pregnant women and nursing mothers are therefore advised not to use it. This is because a high intake of licorice can lead to early delivery and increase the chances of a miscarriage.

Since it causes hormonal imbalance, people with hormone-sensitive conditions are cautioned against using it. It acts like estrogen in the body which can make conditions affected by estrogen worse.

People who have heart diseases should not use licorice as it makes the body retain water and this can lead to congestive heart failure.

Individuals with high blood pressure should also not use it because it worsens the condition since it also raises blood pressure.

People who have hypokalemia are advised to not use licorice. Hypokalemia is a condition that results from low potassium levels in the body, licorice may worsen the condition.

Men who have sexual problems should also not use licorice as it will worsen their problems.

Individuals who are scheduled for surgery should also avoid licorice two weeks before the procedure as it may make it hard to control blood pressure during and after surgery.

Interaction/Reaction

Licorice interacts with many drugs. Examples;

Antihypertensive medications - It reduces the effectiveness of antihypertensive drugs. These are drugs used to control high blood pressure. Licorice increases blood pressure. Examples are losartan, valsartan, furosemide among others.

Warfarin – this drug is used to reduce blood clotting. Taking it alongside licorice reduces its effectiveness.

Ethacrynic acid – these are drugs that lower potassium levels in the body. Taking them with licorice may further lower potassium levels.
Corticosteroids – medications for treating inflammations also lower potassium levels, taking them with licorice can be bad for the body.
Medications broken down by the liver- Licorice increases how fast the liver breaks down certain medications and this can worsen side effects of the liver medications hence one should not take the two together. Examples of these drugs are phenobarbital, ketamine, and secobarbital.
Diuretics – Diuretics are water pills. Some diuretics decrease potassium levels hence when taken with licorice can lead to too much decrease in potassium levels.

Chapter 8 - Milk thistle

Scientifically known as Silybum merianum, milk thistle is a herbal drug commonly used to maintain liver health. It is known to have silymarin which contains anti-inflammatory and antioxidant properties. Here are the benefits of milk thistle;

Benefits

The herb helps to treat liver problems through detoxification. It prevents toxic substances from attaching themselves to the liver. A study done in Finland showed that silymarin helps to treat people with subacute liver diseases. It reduces the liver enzymes that cause subacute liver diseases enabling them to function better.
Research has proven that several people who suffer from chronic hepatitis use milk thistle to help soothe the symptoms. Patients felt much better after taking milk thistle, though it does not exactly treat the diseases.
It is also known to alleviate symptoms in people suffering from type 2 diabetes. When milk thistle is taken for about a month, it reduces inflammation and releases antioxidants that greatly help people with type 2 diabetes.
Silymarin also has neurological functions due to its antioxidant and anti-inflammatory qualities. It helps to prevent the brain from deteriorating due to age.
Milk thistle also helps to prevent bone loss, a condition known as osteoporosis. People who suffer from osteoporosis have really weak bones that can get damaged or break easily. Milk thistles help to add minerals to the bone making it much stronger.

Applying certain milk thistle products can help to treat radiative effects on the skin after cancer treatments. It reduces the effects of radiation especially in women who have undergone breast cancer treatment.
Early research also shows that taking fertility hormones with milk thistle increases the chances of pregnancy in women who are undergoing in vitro fertilization

Side effects
Milk thistles have a few possible side effects to taking it. Some of the common side effects are;
Diarrhea
Bloating on the stomach
Migraines
Nausea
Excessive gas in the stomach.
Other people may experience joint and muscle pain
Some men may also suffer from erectile dysfunction.
In some worse scenarios, one can go into anaphylaxis shock after taking milk thistle if they are allergic to it or daisies, ragweed, kiwi, or any plant belonging to the aster family. Possible allergies are exhibited through swelling (face, arms, tongue, neck), increased heartbeat, dizziness, hives, falling short of breath. These symptoms should be treated immediately as they can lead to cardiac arrest or respiratory failure.

Drug interactions
Medications changed by the liver – milk thistle decreases the effectiveness of how the liver breaks down certain medications. This causes the medications to take a long time to work in the body. Examples include; ibuprofen, warfarin, phenytoin, celecoxib, etc.
Estrogens – milk thistle decreases how effective est5rogen pills are in the body because it decreases hormones. Examples of estrogen pills include Ethinyl estradiol and Premarin
Antidiabetics- Milk thistle interacts with medications for treating diabetes. This is because it already helps to lower the blood glucose level hence when taken with diabetes medication, it can lead to hypoglycemia (when the blood sugar level goes too low).
Cholesterol-lowering medications – it changes cholesterol medications and this can either decrease or increase the effectiveness of the drug. Examples are lovastatin, rosuvastatin, and pravastatin.

Hence, one should not use it alongside antibiotics (clarithromycin), nonsteroidal anti-inflammatory drugs (diclofenac, ibuprofen, celecoxib),

Chapter 9 - Curcumin

Most people have heard about the health benefits of turmeric. Curcumin is the main ingredient present in turmeric. In many studies about the health benefits of turmeric, curcumin properties are usually the heart of the study. It is the yellow pigment that gives turmeric its bright color. The benefits of curcumin are numerous. Here is a list;

Benefits

First, it helps to alleviate pain in individuals suffering from arthritis (osteoarthritis and rheumatoid arthritis). It contains anti-inflammatory properties that help to relieve symptoms such as swelling, pain in the joints, stiffness, and redness.

Secondly, it helps in treating certain eye disorders and prevents some eye disorders from deteriorating.

Thirdly, it can help to treat certain allergy symptoms such as itching, congestion, and runny nose. One can also consume curcumin to help relieve the effects of hay fever. Additionally, people who have had long-term kidney diseases can use curcumin to treat itching side effects.

Fourthly, the antioxidants present in curcumin can be beneficial in treating kidney injuries. It is therefore good for maintaining your kidney health.

Five, it helps to reduce the number of blood fats, this, in turn, manages high cholesterol levels. It does this by lowering triglycerides.

It also helps to relieve the pain experienced after a surgical operation. Curcumin helps to reduce post-surgery pain, fatigue, and swelling.

Lastly, it helps to manage injuries caused to the liver that is not caused by alcohol. By consuming curcumin, it prevents fats from building up in the liver.

Side effects

Curcumin contains a few health risks.

It prevents the body from absorbing iron, which can eventually lead to iron deficiency. When the body lacks iron, the substance that helps the red blood cells to transport oxygen becomes insufficient and this can cause shortness of breath and possibly dizziness.
In men, it can decrease testosterone levels by slowing down sperm movement. This can eventually cause fertility issues.
Some people may also experience nausea, diarrhea, and stomach upset when they take curcumin.
If you are in any of these states, curcumin is probably unsafe for you;
For people who have gallbladder issues such as bile duct obstruction or gallstones, turmeric can worsen the situation.
People with bleeding disorders. It also causes blood clots which might increase the risks of bleeding.
Pregnant and nursing women are advised not to use curcumin as it leads to an iron. deficiency which prevents enough oxygen from reaching every part of the body. Additionally, people who are trying to get pregnant should stay away from curcumin. It reduces testosterone levels in men making it hard for sperm to move.
Women who have hormonal conditions such as ovarian cancer, breast cancer, endometriosis, and fibroid are also cautioned against using it because it worsens these conditions.
Those planning on going for surgical procedures are also advised against using it and it might cause excessive bleeding during the operation.

Drug interactions
Anticoagulants - Curcumin should not be taken alongside anticoagulants like naproxen, enoxaparin, aspirin, warfarin, heparin because it slows down blood clotting. and any other drug that falls under the nonsteroidal anti-inflammatory drugs (NSAIDS). Curcumin causes blood clots, taking it alongside drugs that also slow blood clotting can cause extra bleeding and bruising.

Chapter 10 - Danshen
The root properties of danshen were traditionally used for medicine by the Chinese. Over time, people have realized the healing benefits of danshen especially when it is mixed with other ingredients or medications. Below are the root benefits of Danshen;

Benefits

For one, danshen helps to improve the circulation of the blood because it widens the blood vessels. This makes it easier for blood to flow to different parts of the body.

Research shows that danshen taken alongside other ingredients can be used to relieve chest pain in people suffering from heart diseases. Studies show that it can increase heart function.

Danshen improves vision in people who have diabetes and also suffer from retinal damage.

Danshen and astragalus when injected into the body daily help to treat liver injuries as a result of liver cirrhosis.

When mixed with other ingredients, it lowers blood pressure especially when taken alongside medicine for blood pressure. It improves the effectiveness of the medicine.

It can also be used to prevent blood clots especially when taken with other medications.

Additionally, when a person suffers a stroke due to blood clots, danshen can be administered intravenously to help improve brain function.

Danshen can also be taken to improve brain function after a stroke due to a brain clot.

Lastly, it helps to reduce the chance of the body rejecting a kidney after a liver transplant.

Side effects

Danshen has its side effects. It can cause itching, lack of appetite, stomach upset, and dizziness. These are only some of the symptoms one can experience. Remember that drugs affect people differently. Ask your doctor, if it is okay to take it.

Who shouldn't take danshen?

Like many other herbal medicines, pregnant women and nursing mothers are advised against using danshen. The effects are yet to be determined but it is best to stay safe.

Those who have bleeding disorders are advised not to use it too because it can cause a blood condition called thrombocytopenia.

It can also make the blood pressure go too low in people who already have low blood pressure, hence people with low blood pressure should avoid taking it.

Doctors also advise against using it two weeks before surgery, discontinue the usage if you plan on having surgery because it can cause excessive bleeding.

Drug interactions

Digoxin - Do not take danshen with digoxin. Both affect the heart and the interaction of the two can be bad as it increases the side effects of the medicines

Anticoagulant- It interacts with anticoagulants and can increase the risks of bleeding because it slows blood clots. Examples are warfarin, enoxaparin, Cataflam, clopidogrel among others.

Danshen may also increase how fast midazolam gets broken down. The two should not be taken together.

Chapter 11 - Cranberry

Most, if not all girls have had a urinary tract infection at some point in their lives. Guess what herbal medicine helps to treat UTIs? Cranberry! The cranberry shrub mostly grows in the bogs or wet areas. Cranberry fruit can be used to make a jelly, sauce, and my favorite, cranberry juice. So what are the benefits of cranberry?

Benefits

It is used to treat urinary tract infections by making the urine too acidic for bacteria to survive.

Taking dried cranberry can also improve the symptoms of an enlarged prostate and reduce biomarkers for benign prostatic hyperplasia.

It also helps to eliminate bacteria in the stomach hence taking cranberry juice can help to heal digestive tract infections.

Cranberry juice is also used to treat the symptoms of the flu.

Older people easily suffer from memory loss, taking cranberry juice consistently for more than a month can aid memory retention.

For people who do not drink alcohol, drinking cranberry juice can help to reduce fats from attaching to the liver.

Cranberry powder capsules help to manage an overactive bladder. It reduces the urge to constantly urinate. Cranberry juice can also be used to treat bad urine smells. Furthermore, it can help to treat bladder irritation after radiation therapy

A study has also proven that cranberry products are good for women who have hit menopause. It helps to keep their health in check especially since they are more liable to suffer heart problems.

Cranberry products are relatively safe for most adults. However, too much of something is always bad for your health. It can cause diarrhea and mild stomach upsets when taken too much. In severe cases, it can lead to kidney stones.

Precautions

Pregnant women and nursing mothers are continually advised against taking cranberry products. Children are advised to take it in controlled amounts.

Those who have an aspirin allergy should not take cranberry as it contains salicylic acid that has similar properties as aspirin.

People who have atrophic gastritis should stay away from cranberry products because they will only worsen the symptoms. It increases vitamin B12 absorption in the body for people with an inflamed stomach lining.

Cranberry products have sweeteners, hence can increase sugar levels in people who have diabetes.

For people who have hypochlorhydria, this is a condition where the stomach acid levels are extremely low. Taking cranberry products can worsen this condition.

It also contains oxalates which when combined with calcium can lead to kidney stones. People with kidney problems should therefore stay away from cranberry products.

Drug interaction

Cranberry interacts with certain medications such as;

Warfarin – cranberry increases the time warfarin stays in the body and this can lead to bleeding.

Medications changed by the liver- Cranberry decreases the effectiveness of how the liver breaks down medications. This can make treating symptoms of a particular disease much slower as it will take longer for the liver to do its work.

Blood thinners as it intensifies their effectiveness. Some of the lists of drugs cranberry can interact with include flurbiprofen, diclofenac, amoxicillin, cefaclor, midazolam, and lastly cyclosporine.

Chapter 12 - Goji berry

Goji berries are native to Asia and are known for their medicinal properties. They are often found in dried or powdered forms and added to a variety of recipes. They have a sweet, slightly sour flavor and a vibrant red hue and have been used in traditional medicine for thousands of years.

Benefits

They are a great source of nutrients, including vitamins and minerals. The fruit is loaded with fiber, iron, and vitamins A and C. Iron is an essential mineral involved in oxygen transport while vitamins A and C play central roles in immune function.

Goji berries have been used in traditional medicine to treat illness and infection and naturally enhance immunity. They can be used instead of other dried fruits in cereal, yogurt, trail mix, and granola. The berry powders and juice blends can be mixed into many drinks, shakes, and smoothies.

The berries have a nutrition value of low-calorie and low sugar options which makes them a good substitute for other dried fruits with higher sugar content and a potential weight loss aid.

The berries have a high level of antioxidants. Antioxidants protect cells against breaking down when they are exposed to elements such as smoke and radiation. This protects your eyes and skin.

Goji berries can help improve sugar tolerance, alleviate insulin resistance, improve and recover cells that help produce insulin, and potentially lower blood sugar.

The berries have often been tied to sexual fertility. A study in rats showed that goji berries significantly improved sexual ability and increased sperm quantity.

Some health claims also state that goji berries can lower blood pressure, reduce arthritis pain, and lower heart risks. Another study claims that goji berries can treat cancer tumors.

Goji berries contain a chemical component called bête-sit sterol which may help decrease the size of overgrown cells and can cause apoptosis, or "cell suicide" in tumor cells.

Side effects

Goji berries have certain side effects;

They may lead one to become hypersensitive to certain things. Goji berries can make one allergic to certain things due to lipid transfer. If you take the berries and experience certain symptoms such as the breakout of hives obstruction of the airways, itchiness, then stop immediately and see a doctor before going into anaphylaxis shock.

They can also lead to hypertension because they lower blood pressure.

Some people have reported experiencing diarrhea after taking goji berries.

Here's a list of people who are more at risk if they take goji berries;

Pregnant mothers are advised to talk to their healthcare providers before taking goji berries due to the concert that it can lead to contracting the uterus. Goji berries are also known to contain betaine which can harm the health of a fetus.

People who are more susceptible to allergies from things like peaches, groundnuts, tomatoes should try to avoid goji berries as it can lead one to anaphylaxis shock.

People who are already on medications to lower blood sugar levels should avoid goji as it can make blood sugar levels drop even further.
People who have low blood pressure levels should not take goji berries as it further lowers the blood pressure.

Drug interactions
Antihypertensive drugs – Goji berries decrease the effectiveness of medications for high blood pressure. Examples include diltiazem, hydrochlorothiazide, valsartan amongst others.
Antidiabetics drugs – Lycium bark further lowers blood sugar levels in the body. When taking together with medications to lower sugar levels, it may drop too low.
Warfarin (a blood thinner), you may want to avoid. Lycium increases the time it takes for warfarin to stays in the body. This can cause excessive bleeding and bruising.

Chapter 13 - Evening primrose oil
Extracted from a native plant of North America (Oenothera biennis), evening primrose oil is named for its yellow blossoms that bloom in the evening. Its oil is rich in Omega-6 fatty acids that are found in gamma-linolenic acid (GLA).

Benefits
Used to treat menopause hot flashes, menstrual cramps, and PMS.
Reduction of inflammation in people with Rheumatoid Arthritis.
Reduction of bone mineral loss (especially in women with post-menopause women).
Provides pain relief for people with nerve pains caused by diabetes.

Side effects
Evening primrose oil may induce miscarriage and premature or intense labor.
Since it can lead to extensive bleeding or reduce blood clotting, people scheduled for surgery should avoid it.
People taking anticoagulants (blood thinners) should avoid it as it can increase bleeding.

Drug interactions
People using anti-clotting drugs – for instance, Fragmin (dalteparin)
Patients using anticoagulants like Lovenox (enoxaparin), Plavix (clopidogrel), Coumadin (warfarin), or heparin.

People using antipsychotic drugs like Permatil (fluphenazine), Compazine (prochlorperazine), Mellaril (thioridazine), Stelazine (trifluoperazine), and Thorazine (chlorpromazine)
Users of nonsteroidal anti-inflammatory drugs (NSAIDs) like Advil (ibuprofen), aspirin, Aleve (naproxen), and Voltaren (diclofenac).

Chapter 14 - Echinacea

A native plant of the Rocky Mountains in the United States, Echinacea is mainly grown for sale for its healing benefits. It is believed that its greatest strength lies in reducing inflammation and enhancing the immune system. Although there is no definite scientific proof of total effectiveness, Echinacea is widely used as a herbal drug for the following illnesses:

Benefits

Effective as preventive medicine for colds.
Helpful in control of flu, bronchitis, and asthma.
Research-backed evidence shows that 40mg or more of echinacea extracts per day helps reduce anxiety.
Mild gum disease healing.
Helpful in people with ADHD.
Used as a remedy for migraines.
Helpful against cold sores/ herpes.
Treatment of burns.

Side effects

Causes allergic reactions in adults and children who are allergic to daisies, ragweeds, or marigolds.
Dry mouth
Headache
Nausea
Vomiting
Stomach pains

Caution:

There are no known side effects of using echinacea while breastfeeding (for children) and while pregnant (for expectant mothers), but expectant and breastfeeding mothers are cautioned against using it.

Drug interactions

It can react with immunodepressants (drugs that lower the immune system) because Echinacea improves the immune system.
Common drugs include cyclosporine (Neoral, azathioprine (Imuran), prednisone (Deltasone/Orasone), basiliximab (Simulect), Sandimmune), daclizumab (Zenapax), muromonab-CD3 (OKT3, Orthoclone OKT3), mycophenolate (CellCept), and tacrolimus (FK506 among others.
It may slow down the way the body processes caffeine, leading to an overload of caffeine in the system.
Medications rely on the liver for processing within the system. These may be slowed down by the Echinacea drug and cause major complications. Common drugs include fluvoxamine (Luvox), imipramine (Tofranil), clozapine (Clozaril), cyclobenzaprine (Flexeril), haloperidol (Haldol), mexiletine (Mexitil), olanzapine (Zyprexa), pentazocine (Talwin), propranolol (Inderal), tacrine (Cognex), theophylline, zileuton (Zyflo) and many others.
It can change the way the body breaks down medication in drugs like estrogens, cyclosporine (Neoral, Sandimmune), lovastatin (Mevacor), clarithromycin (Biaxin), diltiazem (Cardizem), indinavir (Crixivan), triazolam (Halcion), and many other drugs.

Conclusion

Herbal medicines are a great alternative to prescription drugs. As helpful as herbal remedies can be, they are not without side effects. When used incorrectly, the effects of herbal medicines on the body can be quite lethal. It is important to research properly about the herbal medicine you plan on taking. If you have any underlying conditions, ensure you consult your doctor before taking any herbal medicine.
One thing that is also important to note: pregnant women and nursing mothers are especially cautioned against taking herbal medicines. Not much is known about how herbal remedies affect pregnancies, so it is better to stay on the safe side. It is also important to recognize the role that herbal medicines play in the treatment of withdrawal symptoms of drug addiction. Prescription medicines come with many side effects, worst of all, addiction. It is never easy to let go of an addiction, people who try experience serious withdrawal symptoms. Herbal remedies are quite effective in helping to treat these symptoms. The greatest wealth is health, to live a good life, prioritize your health.

The most important thing is that you should be informed on not only the benefits but the possible side effects and complications that may arise from any herbal drug you take. You should also inform your doctor about those drugs because not doing so could be the difference between getting well and further complicating the situation.

www.ingramcontent.com/pod-product-compliance
Ingram Content Group UK Ltd.
Pitfield, Milton Keynes, MK11 3LW, UK
UKHW022008190726
13853UKWH00004B/1814